SUNSET STRIP
SUZIE MILLER

CURRENCY PRESS
SYDNEY

[ ] the
uncertainty
principle

GRIFFIN
INDEPENDENT

The writer's royalties for this publication are donated to the McGrath Foundation.

In purchasing this play and program you have contributed to placing specialist breast cancer nurses in hospitals – a much needed resource and comfort for women living with breast cancer.

McGrath
Foundation

In loving memory of Leonie Zurnamer.
Your humour, wisdom and courage still give us strength,
guidance and so many laughs.

'Courage is found in unlikely places.'
— *J.R.R. Tolkien*

'There is no value in life except what you choose to place
upon it and no happiness in any place except what you bring
to it yourself.'
— *Henry David Thoreau*

CURRENCY PLAYS

First published in 2017
by Currency Press Pty Ltd,
PO Box 2287, Strawberry Hills, NSW, 2012, Australia
enquiries@currency.com.au
www.currency.com.au

in association with The Uncertainty Principle and Griffin Independent

Cataloguing-in-publication data for this title is available from the National
Library of Australia website: www.nla.gov.au

Typeset by Dean Nottle for Currency Press.
Cover photograph by Belinda Mason.

Currency Press acknowledges the Traditional Owners of the Country on which
we live and work. We pay our respects to all Aboriginal and Torres Strait
Islander Elders, past and present.

Contents

Sunset Strip was first produced by The Uncertainty Principle and Griffin Independent at The SBW Stables Theatre, Sydney, on 14 June 2017, with the following cast:

PHOEBE	Emma Jackson
TEDDY	Simon Lyndon
RAY	Lex Marinos
CAROLINE	Georgina Symes

Director, Anthony Skuse
Assistant director, Graeme McRae
Producers, Kate Armstrong-Smith and Laurence Rosier Staines
Set and costume designer, Emma Vine
Lighting and projection designer, Verity Hampson
Sound designer and composer, Benjamin Freeman
Stage manager, Gayda de Mesa

CHARACTERS

PHOEBE, about 36, beautiful, fragile, impulsive, charismatic, a single mother whose children are not with her

CAROLINE, about 38, Phoebe's older sister, a lawyer who lives in the big city, clever, serious, in control

TEDDY, two years older than Caroline, Phoebe's lover, a small-town musician, has come to a certain peace with his own demons

DAD (RAY), 60s, once a success in the local mine, he would fish the lake on weekends for its multitude of fish; now has dementia, yet on occasions is lucid and capable of a deep knowing of his situation

SETTING

Sunset Strip: a holiday area of shacks built around a dying lake in New South Wales, just outside Broken Hill. Families once holidayed there but now the lake has completely dried up and the homes surround a dust bowl.

NOTES TO DIRECTOR

Do not be afraid to make parts of the play funny—even silly at times!
While much of it is a coping strategy, the cancer jokes and the irreverence with which cancer and dementia are treated is done as a way of allowing us to be connected to such life events, rather than them being 'other' to our own lives. There is a deep underlying respect for the characters inherent in the work.

/ indicates interrupted dialogue.

This play went to press before the end of rehearsals and may differ from the play as performed.

ACT ONE

SCENE ONE

Afternoon light

Shack

No birdsong

This is 'Sunset Strip'

Once a mecca for holidaymakers to bathe in the lake's clear waters

Now an almost-deserted dust bowl

Miners' families flocked here for years, but children's laughter, swimming, fishing and boating have now all disappeared

PHOEBE *walks in and out turning light switches on and off*

She puts music on

She dances and sings alone and with expression in a 1950s kitchen

Behind her is a tank with two goldfish

CAROLINE *walks up the path with her wheelie luggage*

At one point she stops, lets go of the luggage, winces at some pain under her right arm

Repositions then starts wheeling the case again

She approaches the back flywire door of a fibro shack

Opens backdoor and watches an unsuspecting PHOEBE *inside*

Smiles

PHOEBE *is dancing*

Sees CAROLINE

Shrieks

PHOEBE: Fuck!
   She's here
   You're here

      No hesitation

Leaps into CAROLINE*'s arms*

Can't breathe
Just can't breathe

Strokes CAROLINE*'s hair*

Still beautiful
Your hair
It's still so beautiful

CAROLINE: [*laughing ironically*] Look at you
What a tan!

PHOEBE: [*making a sad bear face*] Was it just terribly difficult to get away?
Of course it was
You poor love

CAROLINE: Where's Dad?

PHOEBE: [*calling out*] Dad!

CAROLINE: [*calling out*] Dad!

PHOEBE: You might find Dad quite … amusing

CAROLINE: Dad?

PHOEBE: You just have to get used to him is all

He's just—
You've been away for so long

CAROLINE: Not by choice Phoebe

PHOEBE: [*rushing in*] No. No of course not

And I would have been over to see you, of course
If things were different
[*Calling out*] Dad Dad Dad!
I would have brought the kids down
Had a holiday

CAROLINE: Hardly a holiday

PHOEBE: Well a holiday from life
And a chance to be there—
With you

DAD *appears*

DAD: Yes
Well I'm here aren't I?

PHOEBE: Look who's here Dad?

> PHOEBE *throws an arm around him and removes some food from his face*

DAD: No need, no need
But I will tell you what I do need
Some nice loin chops
That's what I do need

> CAROLINE *was moving toward an embrace, but how? Not sure*

PHOEBE: It's Caro Dad
Caroline. She's come over from the city
To see us
She's here for a stay

> DAD *steps back*

CAROLINE: So great to see you looking so well
God I've really missed you
PHOEBE: Isn't it great?
Dad

> DAD, *unsure, then recovers*

DAD: And some of that nice asparagus
That would help as well
No time for tea-breaks now my love
CAROLINE: Okay?
PHOEBE: What a great idea, chops and asparagus
Isn't it great to see Caro Dad?
Caroline

Back in the old house
DAD: The old house
Have you told your daughter to come for dinner?

> *Weird silence*

CAROLINE: Dad?
It's me
Caroline

Dad?

DAD: Caroline

CAROLINE: Yes me!

PHOEBE: Your daughter

DAD: I know that

CAROLINE: [*relieved*] Thank God I thought you were being a bit
dippy /

DAD: I know who my daughter is

PHOEBE: 'Course you do Dad

DAD: She lives in the city, in town
Very successful she is, isn't she?

> PHOEBE *'s been there before*
>
> *Tries to have fun with it*

PHOEBE: Yes Dad, sooo successful
She's a lawyer in town isn't she Dad

CAROLINE: ——

DAD: She's my clever daughter

> PHOEBE *finds this so funny*

PHOEBE: I know she's the *clever* one isn't she Dad
And the beautiful one
She's the wonderful sister of the two

DAD: Oh yes
She's very clever yes
But as for …

PHOEBE: Phoebe

DAD: Her mother here thinks the world of her

CAROLINE: [*to* PHOEBE] What's going on?

PHOEBE: I told you it was … different
He's like this one minute and the next he's right back in the land
of now

CAROLINE: But—
He doesn't even know me

PHOEBE: He will
Don't worry

DAD: So chops and asparagus

PHOEBE: Asparagus

DAD: Tell the girl

> [*To* CAROLINE] Did you get that?
> I must go
> I have so much work to finish

CAROLINE: Work? What work?

DAD: Deal with the miners

> They're all in a fluff about some strike

> *He leaves*

PHOEBE: Some days he still goes to the mine even though a) it isn't there anymore! And b) he hasn't actually moved from out the back
He comes home full of news of this one and that one

> It used to make me sad, but now I see the funny side
> [*Laughing*] We have these whole discussions about Bill Parker's car troubles and Mordy's problems at home. It cracks me up

CAROLINE: It's not funny

> You never told me he was this bad

PHOEBE: I didn't want to worry you with that

> You had so much to think about
> And really …

> I mean 'chops and asparagus'
> He does amuse me no end

> *They laugh,* CAROLINE *awkwardly*

CAROLINE: It's awful

> He doesn't even know who we are

PHOEBE: I'm sorry Caro

> It must be a shock
> Of course

> But he has his good days too, don't worry

CAROLINE: You were laughing at him

PHOEBE: [*a threat?*] I live with him Caroline

CAROLINE: It's just not funny

PHOEBE: So what is it then? Tragic?

> You think I don't know that?

> *Silence*

You should have seen them assessing him
I was hoping it might be a good day
But—
He was at his worst
Thought one of those stuck-up slags was the old bat that used to
live across the road

> *Tries not to laugh*

She was beside herself
He was so … 'affectionate'!
'Inappropriately so'

Serves her right
She was a right old cunt
CAROLINE: [*laughing*] Phoebe please

> *Beat*

PHOEBE: [*instantly serious now*] They took my kids Caro

My babies
They took them and then came in here and, and
Had the cheek to look at me like that
CAROLINE: I know
I know
But—
PHOEBE: But? But? But?
CAROLINE: But nothing
Of course nothing
Nothing
PHOEBE: Won't even tell me where they are
Who's with them Caro?
I mean what psycho stranger has my kids?
My kids!
They didn't even take Lila's blanky
She can't sleep without it
She'll cry and no-one will know why
CAROLINE: Shhh shhh
It's all going to change now
You've done everything right

All they said
Completely by the book
You're doing so well
Right?

    PHOEBE *nods*

And now I'm here
PHOEBE: Thanks so much for coming
    For being here

    You know I would have come to town for you
    When you needed someone
    If I could have, you know …
    I would have been there in a heartbeat
CAROLINE: I know /
PHOEBE: In a heartbeat
CAROLINE: Of course
PHOEBE: But with all this
    The—
    And the restrictions and the people I had to check in with /
CAROLINE: It's okay
PHOEBE: But everything's good now—with you—
    Isn't it. [*It's a statement rather than a question*]

    CAROLINE *nods*

Just a really bad memory, hey?

    Silence

CAROLINE: I'll take him out on the boat tomorrow
    He might—
    Maybe that will jolt him back
PHOEBE: Yeah do that
    Take him out on the boat!
    Just the two of you
    Only ones on the lake
    Just like old times

    CAROLINE *is grinning, teasing*

CAROLINE: What—?

CAROLINE *smiles but doesn't understand*

PHOEBE: I tried to tell you
You never take me seriously do you?
Well come
Take a look out the back!

CAROLINE *goes to roll up the blind*

Outside is just a dirt bowl—no water anywhere

CAROLINE: Jesus Christ!
PHOEBE: I told you!
CAROLINE: I thought you were lying!
PHOEBE: Hey?!
CAROLINE: Exaggerating
God it's terrible
PHOEBE: S'pose
CAROLINE: So much worse than you said
PHOEBE: [*shrugging*] Used to it now
CAROLINE: It's just all gone
PHOEBE: Kids still play out on the sand
CAROLINE: Dirt!
PHOEBE: They don't know any different
CAROLINE: Phoebe!
PHOEBE: They're all too young
They don't even remember the lake
CAROLINE: The lake!
There's just nothing there—
PHOEBE: No, no. You're wrong
Not nothing
There's lots of … space

PHOEBE *giggles*

CAROLINE: Why do you stay?
PHOEBE: What do you mean?
CAROLINE: I mean what's the point?

Because the whole reason this house is here
All the houses are here—
Is for the lake

PHOEBE: It's not so bad
    Remember the crowds in summer?
    So now …
    We have the place to ourselves
CAROLINE: How did this happen?
PHOEBE [*shrugging*] Partly because the bloody government's damming
    the river upstream
    Partly a long dry spell
    Volcano in Iceland
    Disposable nappies
    Who knows?
    I'm used to it myself
CAROLINE: It's so empty
PHOEBE: It'll fill up again one day
CAROLINE: What does Dad think?
PHOEBE: You saw him Caro

    Beat

    And anyway, that's the beauty of Dad now
    He doesn't worry about things like he used to!

    He still carries on that he's about to go fishing in it
    Catch a bass or cod!
    Spends hours preparing and then sitting out there

    The rest of the time he spends training these guys

    She looks at the two goldfish

    Coca-cola and Fanta
CAROLINE: Training them?
PHOEBE: On the glockenspiel
CAROLINE: The what?
PHOEBE: The glockenspiel
CAROLINE: They're goldfish
PHOEBE: See this rope, attached to the lever
    He's trying to get them to play a tune

    She taps the tank

    If they move the rope they get the food

Spends hours at it
Music lessons. He read something somewhere

They both laugh

CAROLINE: [*laughing but horrified*] It's not funny Phoebe

PHOEBE *has a big grin as something occurs to her*

Something fabulous

PHOEBE: I have the biggest surprise for you
You have no idea how wonderful
After supper
I just can't wait
CAROLINE: What kind of surprise
PHOEBE: A delicious sumptuous surprise!
CAROLINE: Sounds great
PHOEBE: Wonderful
Everything's wonderful
Now that you're here

Let's take your bags to your room
Show me all the lovely clothes you have bought me from town
I know you have
CAROLINE: I'm hoping you like them
My taste is not as … creative as yours
PHOEBE: [*delighted*] See you did
I told Dad
Wait till Caro gets here
I'll look a goddam treat
Rocking 'Sunset Strip'
That'll be me

Jesus I'm so glad you're here

And—
Sorry to hear about Paul

CAROLINE *doesn't want to talk about it*

Beat

Come see your room
I've decorated it with bunting

CAROLINE: Bunting?

PHOEBE: Yes really!

You can tell I've had so much to do while we've been waiting for you

I mean—bunting!

Come

SCENE TWO

Night

CAROLINE *enters with a purpose*

TEDDY *has been sitting nearby*

Unnoticed by CAROLINE *he watches her*

He has a guitar in a case

Some time passes

CAROLINE *sees* TEDDY

CAROLINE: Shit!

TEDDY: Hi

> *She stares at him, does she recognise him? Ambiguous*

CAROLINE: What are you doing here?

TEDDY: —

CAROLINE: Where on earth did you come from?

TEDDY: [*smiling*] Well I've just been over near Broken Hill

Did a gig over at one of the new mines

CAROLINE: Right

TEDDY: Playing for the troops!

Been a long bloody drive

Just dirt for miles

CAROLINE: Is there something I can help you with?

TEDDY: No

> *Beat*

City clothes hey?

CAROLINE: Sorry?

Look I don't know what / you're [doing here]

TEDDY: Oh she hasn't told you yet
Great
[*calling out*] Phebe?

> PHOEBE *bounces in*

> *She's wearing a new dress*

PHOEBE: Teddy!

> *Silence*

> *Wraps her arms around* TEDDY

Surprise!

> CAROLINE *looks confused*

Teddy, Caro
Caro, you remember Teddy from the servo?
CAROLINE: This is your surprise?
PHOEBE: [*delighted*] My beautiful surprise
TEDDY: Nice to see you again Caro
CAROLINE: It's Caroline
PHOEBE: [*there's a coolness, why?*] Teddy and me
He's come to live with us
With me
And the children when they come home
CAROLINE: ——
PHOEBE: I know it's a——
After all that shit I went through with Javier

What an arsehole

And here he is
My angel

He was right here in Sunset Strip all along

> *She kisses him*

> *They are the only ones in the room*

> *They finish*

> *Silence*

[*Sashaying*] Look! Look at me

TEDDY: Beautiful. Stunning. Sensational!

PHOEBE: Caro bought it for me
From the city!

I cut the dress down a bit though
Is that okay darling girl?

CAROLINE: —

PHOEBE: Oh don't be cross
I adore it
Look
It's so sexy now

TEDDY: Super sexy

CAROLINE: Does Dad know?

PHOEBE: About the dress?

CAROLINE: [*motioning to* TEDDY] Him moving in

PHOEBE: Sometimes!

Laughs

Isn't she beautiful?
Tedds
Isn't she?
Just like I said?

TEDDY: Like sister like sister

PHOEBE: No Caro's always been the good one
The beauty and the brains
And that gorgeous fucking hair
I always had shit hair
Remember that time Caro
That time I dyed my hair pink?

CAROLINE: —

PHOEBE: [*teasing*] Come on you remember?

All the fuss
You remember

CAROLINE: Yes
Okay

TEDDY: Pink!

PHOEBE: Just before I left school
Well, left school on invitation

CAROLINE: Phoebe

PHOEBE: Mum was wild
   Dad was furious
   And you wouldn't talk to me for weeks

CAROLINE: Phoebe

PHOEBE: I embarrassed you!
   You hated it
   Wouldn't let me walk to school with you
   I loved it, made me feel free
   Bright fucking pink!

CAROLINE: No. Yes. Yep

TEDDY: You've arrived just in time

PHOEBE: [*quickly*] Just in time for Lila and Finn's homecoming

TEDDY: Right

CAROLINE: There's something else?

PHOEBE: A party
   Thought we'd have a party to celebrate

CAROLINE: Oh. Yes

TEDDY: Our wedding

CAROLINE: —

       A long beat

PHOEBE: Teddy!
   I wanted to make more of an announcement
   To build it up

TEDDY: Sorry

CAROLINE: Yes

PHOEBE: [*attention back on* CAROLINE] I'm so glad you're here for it
   And Teddy's delighted

TEDDY: I am delighted

CAROLINE: I'm sorry I just didn't know anything about this
   / I thought—
   Phebes, can we—

PHOEBE: And you will be my bridesmaid
   Day after tomorrow
   Before the children arrive—a lunchtime wedding!

       TEDDY *looks at the ground*

CAROLINE: I think I'm in a bit of shock
PHOEBE: [*delighted*] I knew you'd get a surprise!

> I'm borrowing a dress for you from Betsy
> You're the same size as her
> Still!
> You lucky thing

>> CAROLINE *is speechless*

>> *Silence*

TEDDY: I'll go out to the car and get the supplies
CAROLINE: [*alarmed*] Supplies?
PHOEBE: Jack and Coke silly!

>> *A long lingering kiss*

>> TEDDY *leaves*

> Isn't he just the sweetest?
> You're going to love him

CAROLINE: I doubt it

>> PHOEBE *laughs, realises she is maybe serious*

PHOEBE: What?
> Caro?
> Are you joking?
> What's wrong?

CAROLINE: You can't marry him
PHOEBE: What are you talking about?
CAROLINE: You heard me
PHOEBE: [*restrained*] I'm not asking your permission

>> *She lights up a cigarette*

> We love each other
> In a way that I used to think wasn't possible
> Before …

CAROLINE: You have children!
PHOEBE: He adores kids
> Such a wonderful role model for Finn
> Helps with Dad
> Dad adores him

CAROLINE: Are you out of your mind?

PHOEBE: [*unsure? mad? defensive?*] Don't do this already Caro

CAROLINE: You just lost your kids!

PHOEBE: I'm fine!

CAROLINE: [*sarcastically*] Oh is that why I have been summonsed
down here

Because you're 'fine'?

PHOEBE: [*measured*] I appreciate you coming Caro

I do

But it's all a big mistake

Red tape

Once Social Services are onto you they never let up

CAROLINE: And so you thought you'd screw up your chances

By hooking up with, with …

PHOEBE: Teddy

CAROLINE: I know his name

PHOEBE: Good because he's here to stay

CAROLINE: I came out here

Despite everything

Left my home, my—

I took leave

I came here for you

Even though you never came to / see me

PHOEBE: Well it's not Teddy's fault I didn't visit

That's mine

And I wish it were otherwise

But I stuffed up

CAROLINE: Again

PHOEBE: And they wouldn't let me leave

I feel awful leaving you alone through it all

CAROLINE: Poor you

PHOEBE: You're alone now

And I've got Teddy?

I understand that /

CAROLINE: For God's sake Phoebe

You think I want someone like him?!

PHOEBE: I think you're lonely
   And now that I have someone
CAROLINE: You think I'm jealous?
PHOEBE: No. It's not that—

   Beat

   After Paul left you /
CAROLINE: I left him

   A moment while PHOEBE *collects herself*

PHOEBE: So now you don't want anyone else to be happy
CAROLINE: You think that, that man, will make you happy?
PHOEBE: Yes
CAROLINE: Like all the others?
PHOEBE: Don't Caro
   You always do this to me
CAROLINE: And I've always been right

   PHOEBE *blows her cigarette smoke out*

   [*Brushing it away*] Don't blow that poison at *me*
PHOEBE: Oh God
   Don't be like this
   Please don't fucking be like this

   Teddy is a good thing for me
CAROLINE: He's not a good thing for you
   He's … he's …
PHOEBE: What?
   Say it
CAROLINE: He's—
   Weak

   PHOEBE *gestures 'What? How would you know?'*

   Look at him
   He's, he's … low-rent Phoebe

   Will PHOEBE *explode or what?*

   Suddenly she laughs hysterically, really finding it funny
   What?

PHOEBE *starts coughing and laughing*

I'm serious

PHOEBE: And what do you think I am big sis?
  The catch of the century?
  The best fish in the sea?

  Beat

He's good to me

CAROLINE: —

  DAD *enters kitchen scratching himself*

DAD: Caroline love

CAROLINE: Dad?

DAD: Teddy said you'd arrived already
  So glad you came
  Here for the wedding are you love?

CAROLINE: Dad
  No
  Actually I'm here for the kids, Dad

PHOEBE: They're staying with their father but they'll be back after the
  party

DAD: Thanks
  I know that

CAROLINE: Their father?

PHOEBE: Shhh

DAD: Caroline honey, it is a total joy to know you're here

  CAROLINE *wraps herself around him*

CAROLINE: You had me so worried before
  I thought—
  Doesn't matter

  Looks at him lovingly, then ...

DAD: You know I always thought it would be you and Paul getting
  married

  TEDDY *reappears*

Teddy my boy

  TEDDY *kisses a delighted* DAD *on the head*

PHOEBE *reaches for his legs*

TEDDY: Hey old man
CAROLINE: Don't call him that!
DAD: Why? I am an old man
TEDDY: A drink?
DAD: Yeah, I'll get it

Silence

DAD *busies himself in the kitchen*

After a while he changes tack

Starts to put things away in strange places

Forks in the fridge etc

CAROLINE *stands there awkwardly*

Before TEDDY *passes drinks around* PHOEBE *holds him back*

PHOEBE *and* TEDDY *start gazing at each other, touching each other*

CAROLINE: It just wouldn't hurt to wait
   I mean if you're set on doing this, this thing, this /
PHOEBE: Wedding
CAROLINE: Can't it wait until the children are settled in?
   And, and surely you want them to meet Teddy first?
PHOEBE: [*laughing*] Meet him! They adore him
TEDDY: Phoebe wants them to come home to a family
CAROLINE: A family?
   Dad? Help me out here
   Don't you think Phoebe and Teddy should wait a while?
   Until the children settle in
DAD: Problem with you Caroline is that
   You think too much
   Your mother and I would never have married
   If we thought it through like you do
   And then you and Phoebe wouldn't even be here

CAROLINE *notices* DAD *putting things in odd places*

Cutlery in the fridge etc

CAROLINE: What the hell are you doing?

PHOEBE: [*to* DAD] Tell Caroline we are all organised for the wedding
Tell her how much the kids adore Ted

> DAD *turns around*

DAD: Love? What are our girls on about now?

PHOEBE: [*immediately responding, knowing he thinks she is his dead wife*] Same old arguments I'm afraid

> DAD *goes to hug* PHOEBE
>
> *He gives her butt a squeeze*
>
> CAROLINE *jumps up to stop him*

CAROLINE: Jesus!

PHOEBE: [*laughing*] Don't worry—it's not me he's after
It's Mum

CAROLINE: It's not funny

PHOEBE: This is just how it is now

> DAD *tends his fish*

DAD: Come on now mate, you're nearly there

PHOEBE: [*to* DAD] I think Fanta is closer to achieving success, she seems to be more alert

DAD: I wouldn't give up on the other one love, he's just biding his time, mark my words he will get there

PHOEBE: [*to the tank*] Come on Coca-Cola

DAD: Oh no I thought Teddy was getting me a Scotch

CAROLINE: She means the fish Dad, the fish

DAD: No didn't catch anything love

PHOEBE: Teddy—drink for Dad

DAD: Teddy I'll take mine as a nightcap in bed

> TEDDY *hands him a glass of Scotch*

C'mon love, walk me to my room won't you
I wish your mother was here
She always said, 'Phoebe will make the most beautiful bride'

> PHOEBE *takes* DAD'*s arm*

PHOEBE: Be with you two in a moment

> *They exit*

Long beat

CAROLINE: What game are you playing?
TEDDY: Listen
    What happened was a lifetime ago
    It's not something I'm proud of
    But I wasn't together back then
CAROLINE: And now you are?
TEDDY: I've been through a lot Caro
CAROLINE: Caroline
TEDDY: I've dealt with my shit
    Made amends
    Or tried to
    I am not that kid anymore
CAROLINE: Why are you doing this?
TEDDY: It's simple
    I fucking adore her

    She's my everything

        CAROLINE *laughs*

    Is that so hard to believe?
CAROLINE: I love my little sister
    Love her to death
    But I know her

    How long will you stick around?
TEDDY: Don't
CAROLINE: Long enough to get her pregnant?
TEDDY: We were kids
CAROLINE: So are you going to tell her or am I?
TEDDY: You just want to hurt her
CAROLINE: She's my sister!

        Beat

    I want to save her
TEDDY: It won't make any difference

        PHOEBE *returns*

        She is more subdued, thoughtful

        Silence

PHOEBE: Lovely old duffer he is
  He had a little weep about Mum not being here for the wedding

  Silence

CAROLINE: Teddy and I were just talking
PHOEBE: Great
CAROLINE: I mean given that you've just come back from the—hostel
PHOEBE: Caro you don't have to talk in code
TEDDY: I know all about the rehab stint
CAROLINE: You do?
TEDDY: She was really brave to do it
CAROLINE: She had no choice
  If she didn't
  The kids never come back
TEDDY: Well she did it and she did well

  PHOEBE *kisses him*

CAROLINE: But you know—
  Fact is it's day by day
TEDDY: She's doing okay
CAROLINE: Truth is she's a, was a / …
PHOEBE: A junkie
  That's the word you're looking for
TEDDY: Jesus
CAROLINE: You're an addict
TEDDY: A bit of support / would be …
CAROLINE: I have supported her
TEDDY: From afar
PHOEBE: No she's right
  I am an addict
  A recovering addict
TEDDY: And where were you?!
PHOEBE: Leave it Teddy!

  Silence

  She would have been here
  If she could
TEDDY: I'm tired
  I'll see you in bed

PHOEBE: But I thought we'd stay up and party?

    TEDDY *leaves*

    Strained silence

    PHOEBE *tries to resurrect the night*

  So a girls' night then

    She opens a bottle

CAROLINE: It's been a long trip

  I'm going to my room

PHOEBE: Okay sure

    CAROLINE *exits*

    PHOEBE *is suddenly alone*

    Sits down and drinks a Jack and Coke

    Raises her glass to the tank, clinks the tank

  Here's cheers to you two

    Looks at her glass

    Sculls it in

SCENE THREE

Outside on lounges

In the sand / dirt

PHOEBE *dressed in a funky bikini, sunning herself*

CAROLINE *sporting a huge hat, reading glasses and fully dressed trying to read a book*

There's an old boat submerged in the sand/dirt

A fishing rod and some magnetic 'fish' or cans scattered about it

The beating heat

Sun umbrella

Bottles of water

It's creepily silent

DAD *walks by*

DAD: Anyone for a dip?

CAROLINE: God he really thinks there's water in the lake?

DAD: There's water everywhere you lazy lot!

Turns the hose on the two of them (or throws a bucket of water or water bottle on them both), laughs

Both girls are squealing

PHOEBE: Stop it

Stop it

CAROLINE: [*she's wet*] Dad

DAD: Told you both to wear your togs!

CAROLINE *tries to rearrange the umbrella so she can get extra shade*

CAROLINE: It's ridiculous to be outside on a day like this

PHOEBE: I could lend you my Speedo one-piece if you want, you'd be more comfortable

CAROLINE: I don't want to bake myself in the sun Phoebe

And you shouldn't either, especially without sunscreen

Anyway, what's the point without the lake?

PHOEBE: Atmosphere?

DAD *sits in the old boat*

He picks up the magnetic rod and starts 'fishing' for the magnetic fish. Every now and then (from this point) he catches one

CAROLINE: Atmosphere?

Here! Listen

PHOEBE: What?

CAROLINE: No birds

PHOEBE: The sun still sets over the lake, remember how beautiful it was?

CAROLINE: The reflection in the water was what made it beautiful Phoebe!

PHOEBE: Well we still have this whole scenic view!

I love the whole look of it

CAROLINE: You mean watching children in swimmers playing in the dirt?

PHOEBE: It's sand!
  Besides my kids love it
  We play just there, on the edge of the / lake
CAROLINE: On the edge of what?!
PHOEBE: [*ignoring her*] Then rush in for a cold shower every twenty
  minutes

>   PHOEBE *smiles in memory of the kids and her doing this*
>
>   *This is a disagreeable thought for* CAROLINE

  Well we have a ball

  —

  Do you remember what fun we used to have when we played here
  as kids?
CAROLINE: There was a lake then
  That's what we came here for
  We sat by *the lake*
  Swam in *the lake*
  Helped Dad fish in *the lake*
  For real fish!

>   *They both look at* DAD
>
>   *He is concentrating hard*
>
>   PHOEBE *looks affectionately at what he is doing*
>
>   CAROLINE *not so much*

PHOEBE: The kids love 'fishing' with Dad
  He takes them 'out' there
  It's great
  They actually catch something!
  Not like us

  All those years in the boat

>   DAD *approaches*

DAD: Here ya go love

>   *He hands* PHOEBE *a magnetic fish*

  See
PHOEBE: Trust me

It's much more fun to actually catch something!

    PHOEBE *puts the 'fish' in her bag*

    Then rummages through and takes out a sheet of paper from
    her bag

I have this for you Caro

    Shows the paper form that she has

When the bitch from Social Services comes around tomorrow
You have to sign this
Then they can bring the kids
CAROLINE: Does it say how long I have to be here?
PHOEBE: No just that you will tell them if I breach all their stupid rules
    You know
    Stay clean
    Don't neglect
    You're a lawyer you'll understand all that shit
CAROLINE: Okay
PHOEBE: The kids'll be so excited that Teddy's their stepdad
CAROLINE: You could wait
    With the wedding that is

    The children might want to be part of it
PHOEBE: No
CAROLINE: Why?
PHOEBE: I just can't wait
CAROLINE: Same old Phoebe
PHOEBE: Stop that

    Silence

You don't see what I see in him
CAROLINE: I heard you two fighting last night
PHOEBE: It's fine
CAROLINE: He left the house
PHOEBE: To cool off
CAROLINE: What's there to fight about when you're about to get
    married?
PHOEBE: I don't want to talk about it

CAROLINE: I remember him from high school
    He's unpredictable
PHOEBE: [*gleefully*] I know
CAROLINE: That's dangerous
PHOEBE: Wait until you hear him play his guitar
    Now that's dangerous
    The way he looks at me when he sings—
    And in bed—
CAROLINE: I don't want to know about it
PHOEBE: [*laughing*] But we always told each other everything
CAROLINE: That's too much sharing
PHOEBE: I like the sharing

    Beat

    Was Paul good in bed?
CAROLINE: I don't know
    Stop it
PHOEBE: You told me he was
CAROLINE: At first
    Things changed …
PHOEBE: Details! C'mon
CAROLINE: No
PHOEBE: Go on tell me
    Pleeese?!
CAROLINE: It's past

    Silence

    Remember we were all the way in the middle of the lake
    I think you were about five or six
    And I yelled out *'Shark'*

    PHOEBE *lights a cigarette*

PHOEBE: I was so afraid it was about to bite my leg off
    You yelled *'Shark'*
CAROLINE: [*yelling*] Shark!
    You were only little but you swam like a bat out of hell
PHOEBE: Like a torpedo—you were trying to grab my legs
CAROLINE: And tell you it was a joke
    Swallowing gallons of water from laughing so much

PHOEBE: And I thought it was the shark at my legs so it just got me
   going faster
CAROLINE: And when we got back
   You were still swimming right through the shallows
PHOEBE: I looked around and it was you
   Not a shark
   You
   Laughing at me like fuck
CAROLINE: You were too young to know there are no sharks in a lake!

   Beat

PHOEBE: Why can't you be happy for me? Caro?
   It would mean the world to me if you were
CAROLINE: I just think he's wrong
   For you
   And for the kids

   You're not thinking about the kids
PHOEBE: I'm a bad mother is that what you're saying
   Rotten bad incapable mother

   Go on say it

   She smokes furiously

   It's not like you would be the first
   I mean join the fucking queue

   Laughs horribly

   How would you know?
   How it feels to fail as a parent

   I love those kids
   I adore them
   They are my fucken reason for staying alive

   You know what Teddy thinks?
   He says you're jealous
   It sounds stupid doesn't it
   You jealous of me
   But he said I have kids and a partner who loves me, adores me

And you …

You don't have those things

Just your stupid job
Sounds like that was more important to you than everything
So—

That's why you lost Paul
CAROLINE: So it's my fault about Paul!
PHOEBE: You said *you* left *him*
    You didn't fight for it
    It's not like that with Teddy and me
    We love in a way that is hard and rough
CAROLINE: Rough is right!
    Fighting through the nights
PHOEBE: No it's not right
    Not rough like that!
    I understand him
    He understands me
    It's not perfect
    We accept that
    And it's real
CAROLINE: What, so I'm not real?
PHOEBE: Maybe not to Paul
    No I think you have a tendency to be
    Not real
    A bit
CAROLINE: You don't know the first thing about us
PHOEBE: You got sick and you pushed him away
    You don't let people be near you
CAROLINE: Stop blowing that fucking smoke in my face!
PHOEBE: You see
    When did you get so damn uptight!
CAROLINE: So now I'm an uptight bitch
PHOEBE: Every time I so much as look at a cigarette you start the high
    moral ground thing
CAROLINE: You think I'm uptight about you smoking in my face
PHOEBE: Yes you are fucking uptight about it

CAROLINE: Has it never crossed your mind to think why?
PHOEBE: Oh please stop playing teacher with me!
CAROLINE: I have *cancer*

> CAROLINE *whips off her wig and throws it at* PHOEBE
>
> *Silence*
>
> PHOEBE *picks up the wig*
>
> *She eventually attempts to stroke the wig—to tame it, soothe it*
>
> CAROLINE *is delighting in the moment*

There that stopped you!
My trump card

> *Silence*
>
> PHOEBE *puts out the cigarette*

PHOEBE: You've had a terrible scare
We all did
CAROLINE: And yet you still didn't come

> *Beat*

They cut off one of my breasts

> *A moment where* PHOEBE *absorbs the impact*

PHOEBE: I never—
Oh no
You didn't—
Oh baby, I'm so sorry

> CAROLINE *pulls out a prosthetic breast from her bra*

CAROLINE: I call her my Right-Hand Woman
But God she makes me sweat
All slippery silicon
Moves around sometimes too
Girlfriend dragged me out dancing one night
Hilarious
Right-Hand Woman ended up under my bra strap
Did a little migration
And went on a dance of her own
Pert little silicon nipple hanging out of the back of my dress

Everyone behind me getting an eyeful

    PHOEBE, *tentative, curious, touches it*

PHOEBE: It feels kind of real

    She takes it and plays with it

Actually better than real!

    CAROLINE *takes it off her and puts it back in*

    Silence

CAROLINE: And when my hair fell out
    Paul couldn't—
    The whole package
    Veins pulsing in my skull
    No eyebrows
    Angry red scar marking me
    Like an arrow to emptiness
    Left breast a lonely lopsided horn
    I could feel it every time he looked at me naked
    Sexless
    The anti woman
    Anti sex
    Anti—
    He would recoil
    From me
PHOEBE: No. No
    He would never do that—
    Look at you—
    You're still
    So fucken beautiful
CAROLINE: Can't you even tell?
PHOEBE: Tell what?
CAROLINE: What's real?
    That's where you always go wrong
    You just can't tell can you
PHOEBE: I don't know what you're saying
CAROLINE: I'm not the person I was

    She leaves

SCENE FOUR

Late afternoon

Hot and humid

Feel the sting in the air

Relentless

CAROLINE *having a late siesta*

DAD *is trying to get the goldfish to hit the rod that will connect to the string to play the glockenspiel*

PHOEBE *dances in with shopping bags, past* DAD *and the fish*

PHOEBE: Any luck?
DAD: Not yet

>   *She waltzes past*

>   *Wakes* CAROLINE *up*

CAROLINE: Oh God what is it?
PHOEBE: Teddy just gave me a stack of money for wedding things
   I've been shopping!
   Look at everything

>   *Dumps everything on the bed*

>   *Jumps on herself*

>   CAROLINE *has no choice but to wake up*

Look at all the bags

I had so much fun

I bought myself a wedding dress for tomorrow
You'll love it
From Vinnies
It's classic

Look

>   *Holds it up*

Only fifty bucks
I'm gonna leave it in your room so he doesn't see it
CAROLINE: It's beautiful

PHOEBE: And I got you all this organic shit from the health food shop
So you can stop ferreting around in the cupboards for
Things you'll never find

And look—for the kids

Holds up a ballerina dress for Lila

Lila
Isn't it divine?
She will adore it
It's so her
I can just see her little face

Finn

Holds up a monster truck

To plough through the sand outside
CAROLINE: Dirt!

PHOEBE goes wild with the truck

Stops

PHOEBE: I'm going to cling to those kids
And fucken spit in the face of anyone who tries to take them
Once they're back I am never letting go

Intensity fades as she picks up another item

And look

A small metal music box

She plays it

It plays 'Love Me Tender'

Remember Mum used to sing this
CAROLINE: No I don't
PHOEBE: Yes you do

She sings along with it

DAD *starts to bop*

PHOEBE *and* DAD *dance together*

CAROLINE: Maybe. Yes. Okay
I remember

PHOEBE: I think you should stay here forever
    Here with us
    As a family
CAROLINE: But don't I only have to stay until—?
PHOEBE: Until I *prove* myself
    But why not afterwards?
    The kids are your family, they adore you
    I adore you

    Teddy will adore you /
CAROLINE: I have a life in the city
PHOEBE: What, your job?
CAROLINE: Amongst other things
PHOEBE: Paul?
    You could tell him to come here
CAROLINE: No
    You know that's over

        Silence

        PHOEBE *waits for* CAROLINE *to go on …*

        She doesn't

PHOEBE: I bought six bottles of champagne
    They're in the fridge for a pre-wedding champagne breakfast
    I think Mum would have liked that
    And
    Da—da!
    Look what I got Teddy

        She holds up a beautiful guitar

CAROLINE: Phoebe!
    It looks expensive
PHOEBE: Yeah I know
    I thought why spend all that money on a wedding dress
    When he can make music for a lifetime
    He's been checking it out at his friend's house for weeks now
    I convinced the guy who owned it to sell it to me
CAROLINE: Very thoughtful
PHOEBE: I got you something as well

I just think it would be fun

You know—
Something different

I hope you like it

>   *Hands* CAROLINE *a wrapped present*

Ooh I'm really nervous
I just thought—
I don't know

>   CAROLINE *opens the present*

>   *It's a pink wig*

CAROLINE: It's—
   A wig
PHOEBE: Do you like it?
CAROLINE: It's—
   It's pink!
PHOEBE: You don't have to wear it
CAROLINE: Thank you
PHOEBE: It's a big 'fuck you' to the world
   A big 'up yours' to the Big C
CAROLINE: I appreciate the sentiment
   Really do
PHOEBE: I promise I will still walk to school with you!
CAROLINE: Did you keep the receipt?
PHOEBE: I just thought
   You deserve to stand out in a crowd
CAROLINE: It's just—
   Not me
   It's more you

>   *Goes to hand it back*

   Get a refund
PHOEBE: No just—
   I don't know
   Keep it

   You look good in pink

CAROLINE laughs

Then PHOEBE *laughs*

It triggers something

And

DAD/RAY *barges in*

He is furious, approaches PHOEBE

DAD: I told you
  I told you not to go
  I said 'Don't go'
PHOEBE: It's okay Ray
  I'm back now
DAD: I told you not to go /

    He is pushing PHOEBE *up against the wall*

CAROLINE: Dad!
PHOEBE: Ray did you catch some fish?
  We need to get them in the fridge, or put them in ice?
CAROLINE: Dad!

    She approaches and tries to get him away from PHOEBE

What are you doing?
DAD: You fucking stay out of this
  She's done it again

    Back to PHOEBE

How dare you
You come in here pretending to be something you're not
I'm calling the police

    He holds her arms behind her back

PHOEBE: I'm sorry Ray /
  It won't happen again
CAROLINE: Dad
  Leave her alone
  Why is he doing this?
DAD: Back off
  You just back off lady

PHOEBE: Caro it's okay

DAD: [*to* PHOEBE] You've done enough damage today

And you've gone and brought her back

Well there's no party here, you hear me?

I'm calling the police

He is less insistent, not physical anymore

PHOEBE: I think the police are at the door Ray

Shall we go and talk to them

Tell them what's happening?

DAD: She shouldn't be on my property

PHOEBE: No

There are laws against that

DAD: Yes laws

The law must be obeyed

PHOEBE: Caroline's here Ray

She's a lawyer shall we get her to talk to the police

DAD: Yes

Of course

Ask Caroline

She's a lawyer

PHOEBE: Great idea

DAD: Tell them I have a daughter who's a lawyer

And she's coming to talk to them

I am writing them a legal letter

PHOEBE: Caro can you talk to the police at the door

I'm just taking Ray into his room and then I'm going to check on the catch

DAD: Yes the fish

Put them on ice for me

PHOEBE: I will definitely get them on ice, and you can have a bit of a lie down

DAD: A lie down

That's a good idea

PHOEBE: [*to* CAROLINE, *quietly*] It's okay

He's never really hurt me

CAROLINE: I've never seen him like this?

PHOEBE: He can't help it Caro
   It just happens

   Come on Ray
   You've been out on the boat all morning
DAD: Yeah
   I'm too old for all this work
   It's time you took over love

     They leave

SCENE FIVE

Evening

TEDDY *and* CAROLINE *hovering*

Uncomfortable

TEDDY *has been drinking*

TEDDY: Drink?
CAROLINE: Where is she?
TEDDY: She's a big girl Caro
CAROLINE: She should be home
TEDDY: Big day tomorrow
   She's got dresses to alter
   Things to pick up
   Lots to organise

   She's excited
CAROLINE: —
TEDDY: Why haven't you ever married?
CAROLINE: Why?
TEDDY: It's a straightforward question
CAROLINE: I have had very serious relationships you know and they—

     Silence

TEDDY: I'm sorry about … things
CAROLINE: No need
TEDDY: Phoebe told me you can't have children
   After the treatment

CAROLINE: Phoebe—
    God
    She had no right to tell you
TEDDY: She was upset you know /
CAROLINE: Anyway it's not something that matters to me
TEDDY: I've been wanting to apologise to you for a long time
    I tend to do a lot of that these days
    Apologise to people
CAROLINE: Yeah well they're just words aren't they
TEDDY: Yes
    But it's all I have Caro

    And now that you—[can't have kids]
    I feel—
CAROLINE: Stop!
    Please don't think for a minute I regret it
TEDDY: Jesus a guy tries to be nice
    To say the right thing
CAROLINE: Not for a moment would I bring up a child with someone
    like you!
TEDDY: You think because you're some big-time city lawyer
CAROLINE: You know
    I'm over this stupid assumption that
    Just because someone's intelligent
    And a lawyer
    Oh dear a *lawyer*
    And mildly successful
    That I'm some sort of judgemental humourless bitch
    I'm really over it
TEDDY: She said 'humourlessly'
CAROLINE: I laugh, I can laugh
TEDDY: I'll bet!
CAROLINE: Truth is I want more for my sister
    Not some hand-me-down

        TEDDY *stands up*

        Fury

TEDDY: Bait me all you want

Silence

You know I don't understand you
Why you're so bitter
CAROLINE: Jesus give me a drink

> TEDDY *pours her a large Scotch, her first for months*
>
> *She downs it quickly*

It had nothing to do with you
TEDDY: How can you say that?
CAROLINE: It wasn't about anything other than
    A mistake
    A big stupid mistake
    One hideous secret summer
    When my life was falling apart
    Dad was shutting down
    He had no idea about Phoebe and me growing up
    Girls becoming women
    Neither did we really
    I was missing my mother so badly

    And you Teddy are just an error of judgement that
    Believe me I have paid out on myself for

    Oh and
    Even literally I paid
    For the fucking termination
    From the money I earned working Christmas holidays at the
    pharmacy
    Bled my way home on a bus
    Okay!
    You weren't even man enough to—
TEDDY: I was a kid
    Scared shitless
    Nineteen for Christ's sake
    People make mistakes Caro
    They fuck up and lose things along the way
    We don't all have the perfect—
    And when they make those mistakes

Fuck up on other people
They know they have done it
So it hurt me too, destroyed some part of me
Knew I was useless, wasted
Guilt becomes anger becomes self-sabotage becomes hatred
All at myself
That's what happens
There are so many ways to fuck yourself over

And I have learnt from that
Yes. I am not that—that boy. Not anymore
CAROLINE: Uh huh
TEDDY: I can love now Caro
   I still have my faults but
   I'm not scared to be honest
   Phoebe and me
   I want you to know
   It's special
   Like suddenly the world is in colour for me
   Never had that before
CAROLINE: You've obviously had a lot of therapy
TEDDY: [*trying to contain himself*] What'd they do to you Caro?
   Slice out your heart when they took off your breast?

      CAROLINE *is shocked*

      Horrified

   That's the real reason your man left you isn't it?
   Hard to hear the truth is it Caroline?
   Half a woman, no heart
   No fucking heart
CAROLINE: [*embarrassed, exposed*] I'm—
   I have to—

      She gathers herself

      Her things

      She has drunk too much

      TEDDY *punches himself*

TEDDY: Shit
    I'm sorry
    Caro
CAROLINE: I need my bag
TEDDY: Fuck
    I'm fucking sorry
CAROLINE: I have to go
TEDDY: Please Caroline
    She told me not to mention—
    I'm sorry
    It's not what I really—
CAROLINE: Out of my way

        TEDDY won't move

        Blocks her

        Holds her there

    Let go of me

        She is crying

        Embarrassed

TEDDY: Oh God

        He wraps her in his arms

        She resists violently

        But loses her energy

        Gives up

    You are all woman
    All woman

        She sobs

    And your breasts
    Your beautiful white breasts
    I still remember them like it was yesterday
    Yes
    You never—
    I remember the curve and cup of them
    The mystery of them /

CAROLINE: Stop it
TEDDY: I'm trying here
CAROLINE: Don't
TEDDY: No
   I'm saying that
   They're still perfect in my memory
   No damage, no scar
CAROLINE: I hate you
TEDDY: Don't you fucking get it?
   Sheer beauty doesn't last
   Nothing like that is real
   It's not perfection anymore
   It's life

   Sometimes what's left behind reminds us
   Of how we survived
   And maybe
   Just maybe
   I don't know

   I'm a fuck-up
   But maybe
   There's some beauty in just surviving
   And feeling the pain

   Life is uncertain for everyone Caro
   Not just with cancer
   Not just for you
   Even when we don't know it
   The pain and worry is everywhere
   You're not made of glass
   You won't break

      CAROLINE*'s eyes are closed*

      TEDDY *is holding her gently now*

      An apology

      A mixed-up sexual advance

      A need for forgiveness

A past arousal recovered

You're still there
Still exquisite

    TEDDY *holds her with some desire*

    Some need

    A confused attempt at what?

    His lips trace the side of her face

    Hands gentle and sensual

    This is all quiet and frightening

    Too much alcohol

    Too much past

    Time passes

    Do they kiss?

    PHOEBE *arrives unnoticed*

    When they realise she is there they jump apart

PHOEBE: [*directly at* CAROLINE] Why do this to me?
    You hate me this much?
    You need to be the best at everything?
    Even this!
TEDDY: Phoebe / stop it
PHOEBE: Now you want some low-rent cock
    Is that it?
    Have a bit of a danger walk

    I fucking hate you
    You hear me

    I fucking hate you!

    She exits with TEDDY *after her*

    TEDDY *stops and turns to* CAROLINE

    But there's nothing to say

    He's the same guy he's always been

Fucking up again

He runs after PHOEBE

CAROLINE *falls to the ground with the wedding dress and shoes*

END OF ACT ONE

ACT TWO

SCENE ONE

Morning

CAROLINE, *sitting by the 'lake'*

Dressed in PHOEBE*'s wedding dress*

And PHOEBE*'s wedding shoes!*

She is filthy

Hasn't been to bed

Has escaped the house

She is slugging from a champagne bottle

On her head is the pink wig

Down from the house comes DAD

He sees CAROLINE

Comes over and sits with her

DAD: You thinking of a swim?
CAROLINE: [*deadpan*] There's no water
DAD: I know, I was having a little joke
CAROLINE: Swim?
DAD: I know—
    I'm not much good to you now am I?
CAROLINE: No. It's fine
DAD: I wish I could look after you

      CAROLINE *realises* DAD *is being his old self*

CAROLINE: I don't need looking after
DAD: There are days that I would swear that this lake had boats on it
    All sorts of craft
    And I can see them
    Watch them forever
    Waiting for them to come to shore

They never do

And then I slip
CAROLINE: Oh Dad
DAD: [*with a sigh*] I envy your mum
    Heart attack seems like a lovely way out
CAROLINE: Yeah
DAD: Your sister's having a screaming row inside with Teddy
CAROLINE: When do the kids arrive?
DAD: This afternoon
    Be lovely to have them back
    The sound of children
    I need them
CAROLINE: —
DAD: When your mum and I first had you
    The delight of you
    Your little fingers curled around mine
    Tiny fists
    Perfect eyelashes
    I felt what they tell you
    That urge
    Fatherly love
    The desire and certainty that I would kill anyone
    Anyone who dared try to hurt you
    Powerful stuff that

    I know I can't save you from things now
    Jesus I can't even leave this place
    Can't leave Sunset Strip
    But I need you to know
    While I can still tell you
    If I could slay the dragons—

    Just need to tell you—
    The desire, the certainty is still there
    The ferocity
    It's just—
CAROLINE: I'm okay Dad
DAD: You're my strong one Caro

CAROLINE: Yes

Silence

No
I'm not your strong one Dad
I'm no-one's strong one
I'm fucking terrified
DAD: Of course you are
CAROLINE: People have changed toward me
I hate it Dad
I don't want pity
I don't fucking want it
Makes me invisible

Beat

I'm sorry Dad, forget it. I'm fine
DAD: Don't be sorry
I need to be your dad
For me as well as for you
To hear it
To know it
CAROLINE: Well I don't know how to live like this
There's no manual
DAD: Too right love
CAROLINE: Only chemo and—
DAD: Oh darling
CAROLINE: Is anything worth striving for
Wishing for?
What does my life look like?
DAD: Sweetheart
Your life is what it is
Not what you might have wished for
But it is the one you have
Find what matters
To you
And hold that tight
CAROLINE: I'm really scared

She cries

He holds her; close, desperate to save her, protect her even though he no longer can

It's not—
I'm not okay Dad

DAD: Things will turn out

CAROLINE: It's in my liver

DAD: Oh darling

CAROLINE: I haven't told Phoebe yet
I was waiting for—

> *She is allowed to really cry*
>
> *As a child, he is there for her, holding his baby*
>
> *She recovers a bit and sits up*
>
> *She looks at him*
>
> *He is slipping away*

DAD: Shall I get your mum?

CAROLINE: Dad—?
Please—

DAD: She'll know what to say

CAROLINE: —

DAD: I'll go up to the house, tell her to come—
Oh look
Here she is now
Read my mind

> PHOEBE *is coming down the sandhill*
>
> DAD *stands up to greet her*

Darling I think it's time for a talk with daughter number one

> PHOEBE *doesn't miss a beat*
>
> *She's used to it*

PHOEBE: You go up to the house Ray
Your toast is on the table

DAD: There you go
She's here

> DAD *leaves*

PHOEBE sits

Notices what CAROLINE *looks like then*

They both look out at the empty lake

Time passes

PHOEBE: Celebrant will be here in an hour
CAROLINE: Wedding still on then?

    PHOEBE *nods*

Phoebe /
PHOEBE: You might think you know Teddy
But you don't

You have no idea
He is a kind, gentle man
I know he's flawed
But I don't believe in perfection
I hate perfection
The chinks in him are lovely to me
His scar tissue made him who he is
So he can't cope sometimes
He's passionate
And unpredictable
But—
And you listen to me carefully Caroline
He is completely mine

I don't expect you to ever understand this
Know how I could choose him
A warm, pained, flawed, difficult man
But I know him
His softness, his nightmares, his self-hatred
I understand that Caro

Teddy and I have travelled to hell and back
And it is nothing noble
Nothing you can blame on chance
On lack of luck
It's purely the fuck-up of who we are

My children are coming home today after being in a stranger's
home
Because their mother was deemed not good enough
A marred mother
Junkie mother
Sneered at by Social Services
A maternal failure
The only real job I've had

But I'm the only one who knows them
Really knows them
I know what song to sing when Lila's scared
Understand when Finn gets anxious
That he needs a big tickle and a hug
I'm their mum
And that counts for something

I don't care what everyone says
Because those two little people
They're perfect
The two things I got right
So I don't need all the judgement
Because together we make
A good little family
The three of us and Teddy

I can't lose them Caro
I will fight to my death to get them back

And Teddy understands
He's seen me with them
Seen me as a mother
Fiercely loving them
Understands I need all of us to be a family
He knows how afraid I am
And he isn't running from my fear
He sees it
And understands it
Because he has it too

He might not be a big city man
And yes he has a past littered with disaster
But all that is nothing
Compared to how I feel about him
How we touch each other

And I don't care about the past
A past that has you in it
I don't care—

He told me everything
Yep
We have no secrets
My only relationship
With no secrets

CAROLINE: He told you everything?
PHOEBE: Why don't you tell me?
I wish we could
You know—
Really talk
Tell me what you've been through
What you're feeling

CAROLINE: When Mum died I did everything
I tried Phoebe
You just sat around feeling miserable

I was a kid
But I had to do all the horrible stuff
And I do it
I always do it
Like it is supposed to me that does it
You're allowed to be a fuck-up

PHOEBE: I don't mean to be
CAROLINE: I even gave you my share of what Mum left us
So you could get ahead
What was it that time?
Pay off your debts
Start a business in town

Why are you allowed to be so irresponsible?
And I never complained
Never

Because you were my little sister
Who always screwed up
PHOEBE: Jesus Caroline
CAROLINE: Because you were funny and warm
And loving
You were 'Phoebe'
And we all had to be there for you
To pick up the pieces /
PHOEBE: We can't all be freaking perfect
CAROLINE: Always
Everything was about jumping to make sure you were okay
And
Just this once
Just this once in my life
I needed you Phebes
To come to me, to drop everything and to—
Just …

I needed to be small
To lean on someone
To be allowed to fall apart
PHOEBE: Oh Caro

> *She reaches out*

CAROLINE: I thought of Mum so often while I sat through chemo
What it was like to be alone and struggling
Fighting her demons
There was so much I wanted to talk to her about

Paul would drop me off and pick me up
He was juggling work and home and …
But me, I was just having cancer

And I felt myself changing
Not just physically
I felt the world differently

Looked at it from another angle
Things that used to seem important didn't matter anymore

Every time Paul looked at me he just looked terrified, tiptoeing
around me
Making me feel fragile and separate
I wanted you, I wanted Mum
I needed you, I needed Mum

But Mum's gone
And you … you weren't there Phoebe

    They sit with this for a moment

There was just this terrifying new loneliness
PHOEBE: Oh fuck
CAROLINE: This one day
    I was just completely overwhelmed with, with …

And I had a nurse
Assigned to me by the clinic
At first with her I was all bravado and … 'being a good patient'
But
I was crap
And she could tell
She sat with me
I couldn't talk to her
Didn't know what to say
But she knew—she just fucking understood

She, Sophia
She, she picked up my hand
And she held it, and she looked right at me
While the tears just … God they just … poured out of me

And it felt good to be seen
Properly seen and understood

    PHOEBE *picks up her hand and holds it*

    She really means it

PHOEBE: I should have been there

I should have been
All the excuses … but I should have fucking just …

Caro
I will do better
I'll do my absolute best

   Beat

I'm glad someone was there
CAROLINE: I told her about you
   Some of our childhood stuff
   It made her laugh

Stories of Dad dragging you home
And that boy—the one you lived in the treehouse with!
PHOEBE: Oh God
   Aaron DeLutis
CAROLINE: Aaron—yes
   Dad and I delivering food up to you via a chain with a bucket
PHOEBE: I survived a whole summer up there
CAROLINE: Where did you shower and / ?
PHOEBE: You don't want to know!

   Beat

Aaron lives in an Ashram in India now
CAROLINE: He does?
PHOEBE: Says I drove him to the silent life of a monk!
CAROLINE: Oh God
PHOEBE: Although I notice he's on Facebook so he might have
   overstated his commitment!

   Laughter

CAROLINE: I'm sorry I've come between you and Teddy
   I'm leaving for the day so you can enjoy your wedding day together
   Heading into town
PHOEBE: In this state
   I don't think so
   You'd blow your reputation to pieces

   They laugh

I am marrying the man I love today
And—
And I want my sister
I want you there
CAROLINE: You couldn't possibly want me there
PHOEBE: I not only want you
I *demand* that you are there

And—

I also will require
When you are ready
And if you could manage to part with them

My wedding dress

And shoes

SCENE TWO

Afternoon after the wedding

Still dressed in wedding outfits

DAD *and* TEDDY *are playing chess*

PHOEBE *and* CAROLINE *are still drinking champagne*

CAROLINE *is still wearing the pink wig*

This time with her bridesmaid dress, badly fitted

CAROLINE: Did you see her face?
PHOEBE: [*glowing*] She was like 'Good God'. 'I guess it's a love-ly
hairstyle'
So sarcastic
CAROLINE: Love-lovely hairstyle!
PHOEBE: And then you—

PHOEBE *can't talk for laughing*

CAROLINE: 'Well of course the hair is the first thing to go' /

PHOEBE *can't resist delivering the punch line*

PHOEBE: 'On chemo'
CAROLINE: She couldn't look at me

PHOEBE: 'On chemo'
   So deadpan
CAROLINE: Self-important bitch
PHOEBE: 'On chemo'

   CAROLINE *and* PHOEBE *piss themselves laughing*

CAROLINE: 'Yes yes I—
   Yes shall we get on with the ummm—'
PHOEBE: And you—
   When she got stuck
   '… *the wedding*, not the funeral today'
CAROLINE: It was the champagne
PHOEBE: 'But if you are doing cut-price, if you could quote / two for one—?'
CAROLINE: Two for one
   I was awful
PHOEBE: Evil
   And totally adorable
TEDDY: Not that one Ray
   Try this one and you get my horse

   DAD *stares*

   TEDDY *moves a piece of* DAD*'s which knocks off* TEDDY*'s horse*

   Dammit you got my horse
   You sneaky old bastard
PHOEBE: That's the way Dad
   Thrash him
DAD: Yes

   PHOEBE *goes up and whispers something to* TEDDY

   He runs his fingers up her legs as he concentrates on the game

   CAROLINE *watches*

PHOEBE: Okay all
   The bride is going to retire to her royal chambers to have a wee nap before the children arrive
   Get myself all cleaned up for the motherhood police
   You got the paperwork ready Caro?

CAROLINE: All organised; I'm ready to sign it
      Can't wait to see the rug rats
PHOEBE: They will be asleep in their home tonight
      Tucked in their own beds
      Home
      With a new dad
      And their aunty
      I'm so excited
CAROLINE: Yep, tomorrow we can go digging in the dirt!

> TEDDY *moves one of* DAD'*s pieces*
>
> *Then one of his own*

      The wedding was—
PHOEBE: Crazy
TEDDY: Best day of my life
CAROLINE: Congratulations

> PHOEBE *and* TEDDY *have eyes only for each other*
>
> *There is real tenderness there*

TEDDY: So I'll join you after the game?
PHOEBE: An afternoon wedding night
TEDDY: Wedding nights for the rest of our lives

> *Unseen by everyone,* DAD *has been pondering the pieces on the chess board*
>
> *He moves a piece*

DAD: Check
TEDDY: What?
DAD: Checkmate
TEDDY: You bugger

> PHOEBE *exits*
>
> TEDDY *realigns the pieces*

      Another game old man
DAD: —

> *Silence*

CAROLINE: So I guess we're brother and sister now

TEDDY: I guess
CAROLINE: Weird
TEDDY: Hmm
[*To* DAD] Hey old man
CAROLINE: He's asleep

She goes over and makes DAD *comfortable*

Are we okay?
TEDDY: You tell me

A moment

CAROLINE: Mistakes
When I was diagnosed
The first thing I felt was that there was a stupid terrible mistake
Or that there was something—
Something I could do to change the results
I felt like I must have done something terribly wrong
That I was asking for it somehow

I didn't tell Paul right away
When he found out he thought—
Thought I didn't want to share things with him
But it was more that—
If I didn't tell him then maybe it wasn't real
That was my first mistake though
Not telling him
Not showing him where I was
I was afraid
Not just of the cancer
I know people who have battled cancer
Survived it for years
I was afraid I would lose him
Not that he would leave
But that I wouldn't be there in the same way
And after they operated things just felt different
The radiotherapy wasn't so bad
But the chemo
It was horrible

I was vomiting and shitting everywhere
I smelt awful
But mainly I knew I was in this on my own
That it was me and my body and no-one else had the same fear
I was the one that was going down not him
Not everyone else

Watching people at the supermarket
They were all just buying bread and orange juice
Chocolate chip cookies
And you know I never thought of myself as a jealous person
Teddy
There were always girls prettier than me
My sister had a bundle of charisma
Best friend was the one with the best boyfriends
I was never jealous of anyone
I was happy being attractive enough, clever enough
But when I was on chemo
I looked at everyone
Old ladies with sticks on the streets
Busy mums hassling their kids to cross roads
Women at the hairdresser
God even fucking parking attendants
And I was jealous of everyone
Every single person
Even my little sister
Who was going through the trauma of losing her kids
I was jealous of everyone

Because they didn't have cancer

And I was especially jealous of Paul
Because he could walk away
And I thought he was weak and stupid for not walking
For staying
I could see the horror when he saw my cut-up body the first time
He tried to hide it, and that made it worse
And when my hair fell out
I could see his fear

Smell his fear
And yet he wouldn't walk
He just stayed
Kept up as if I was still me
Still complete

But he couldn't touch me
TEDDY: Doesn't mean he didn't want to

> *They meet somewhere*

> *There is something real happening*

He was probably just scared
Do you love him?
CAROLINE: —

> *Starts searching for something in the drawers*

I used to cycle all around these parts when I was a kid
Phoebe and I—wind in our hair

> *Finds what she is looking for—a bicycle pump*

Same old pump
A hundred years old
TEDDY: You should be with him
CAROLINE: What?
TEDDY: Paul

> CAROLINE *looks right at him*

CAROLINE: Too late
I'm needed here now
TEDDY: —
CAROLINE: Do you know where the old bikes are?
TEDDY: What?
CAROLINE: I want to take the kids out
Riding with the wind in our hair!
Well at least in their hair!

> *Silence*

I might go and pump up the tyres
Are the bikes still under the house?

TEDDY: No
CAROLINE: They haven't been thrown out have they?
TEDDY: No
CAROLINE: Is everything okay?

>   *A moment of contact,* TEDDY *makes a decision*

TEDDY: They're in the shed
    Round the back
CAROLINE: Thanks

>   *They meet again*

>   TEDDY *looks away*

    Be back in a sec
TEDDY: Good luck

>   CAROLINE *is confused*

CAROLINE: Okay

>   *There is something else that* TEDDY *wants to say but he doesn't say it*

TEDDY: I'm off to bed

>   *She leaves,* TEDDY *watches her then goes himself*

>   DAD *is still there, sleeping*

SCENE THREE

PHOEBE *is in the shed*
She is prepping a place between her toes
A needle at the ready
CAROLINE *carries a pump in and sees* PHOEBE *poised for action*
Silence

CAROLINE: My God
PHOEBE [*continuing with the needle*] It's just a once-off
CAROLINE: A once-off?
PHOEBE: Just to get my nerve up
CAROLINE: I'm not Mum Phoebe
    I know what this means

PHOEBE: I can handle it Caro

CAROLINE: Lila and Finn

PHOEBE: I'm so nervous

Just needed some Dutch courage

CAROLINE: You never stopped did you?

PHOEBE: I went to rehab

CAROLINE: And learned nothing

PHOEBE: Don't be like that Caro

You understand

I get so stressed about things

Get so worried I'm going to fail

So scared I'll disappoint my babies

CAROLINE: They have been in foster care all this time

Waiting for their mum to come

PHOEBE: It's just to get myself ready for them

I need to be prepared

CAROLINE: Missing you

And look at you—

PHOEBE: I am who I am Caroline

Loving them is who I am but this is part of me too

I can't live like other people

But it doesn't make me a terrible mother

I adore those kids

I love them more than anything

CAROLINE: Then stop this shit Phoebe

Love them without this

PHOEBE: I will I will

CAROLINE: —

PHOEBE: This is my last shot I promise you

CAROLINE: Does Teddy know?

PHOEBE: As long as I don't lose control with it he's cool

CAROLINE: You've already lost control

PHOEBE: No. No I haven't

I can function completely fine with this much

You've seen me

CAROLINE: And tomorrow it's this much then this much then this and /

PHOEBE: No, tomorrow I give up because I'll have got my kids back

CAROLINE: That's not how it works Phebes
　　You know that
　　Surely you know that

　　They'll never give you your kids if you / keep—
PHOEBE: They will never know
　　Don't need to know
　　It's all a terrible mistake
　　I love my kids
　　I love my babies
　　I would do anything for them
CAROLINE: Except the one thing that brings them home
PHOEBE: They'll still come home
　　Why would they not come back?
CAROLINE: [*shaking her head*] Why?

　　　Looks at the needle

　　Tell me Phebes why?
PHOEBE: I don't know
　　It's not like I want it to be like this
　　I adore my children you know that don't you?
CAROLINE: Yes I do know that
　　I believe that
　　But you—
PHOEBE: Fuck

　　You're not going to tell them …

　　You're going to tell them aren't you?
　　You'd do that to me? No? You—
　　Oh God
CAROLINE: I have no choice
PHOEBE: Oh God
CAROLINE: How could I let the kids come back with you—?
PHOEBE: Oh God
CAROLINE: How could Teddy let you do this?
PHOEBE: Please Caro
　　You can stay and see I will be fine with them
　　You'll sign the document

You'll be allowed to supervise

CAROLINE: You've been using the whole time I've been here?

PHOEBE: And you'd never know right?

I'm completely normal

Like Mum with her benzos

CAROLINE: Christ

PHOEBE: Just this chance

You're my beautiful sister

You'll be here

I'll change

You can take it all away

CAROLINE: I can't sign the document Phoebe

PHOEBE: Yes you can

CAROLINE: What if something happened to the children?

I'd never forgive myself

PHOEBE: Nothing will happen

You trust me?

CAROLINE: I don't trust the drugs

PHOEBE: Please

Okay, I won't ever do it again

I promise

You can sign it

CAROLINE: I'm a lawyer!

PHOEBE: You're my sister!

CAROLINE: —

PHOEBE: What about Lila and Finn?

You going to leave them in foster care?

With some crazy family who'll abuse them?

You want that for my kids?

Because they won't let *you* have them

Not while you're sick

They need to come home

Teddy's here, I'm here, Dad, you—

CAROLINE: You're their fucking mother!

PHOEBE: I'm begging you

Live here with us, you can check all the time /

CAROLINE: You're their mother Phoebe
PHOEBE: I know

> *Silence*

Fuck you
If you can't do this for us—
For me
For my children
Then fuck you

Jesus please just sign the fucking document

> *Realises* CAROLINE *is not going to sign the document*

> *Quiet tears*

CAROLINE: I should go
Back to the city
PHOEBE: —
CAROLINE: I'll leave Betsy's dress on my bed

> *Silence*

PHOEBE: Shall I come and see you?
CAROLINE: One day
PHOEBE: I will, I swear

> *Silence*

> CAROLINE *turns to leave*

> *She gets quite far*

You know
That day
With the shark in the water
I wanted to save you

I could hear you
Behind me
Screaming
So loud
Screaming
Shark
Shark

So I swam like mad

I could feel the shark brushing up against my legs
But all I could think
Was 'the faster I swim
The further I take it away from you'

I didn't care about myself
I just knew I couldn't let the shark kill you

I didn't care if it got me
If I had to choose, I knew that
My life wasn't worth living without you

I loved you so much

I never told you
Never told anyone
I thought I had saved your life

When I got to shore
I was exhausted
But mostly I was thrilled
It was the proudest moment in my life
I had protected the one person I truly loved

I'd done it
And it was the most incredible thing I'd ever done

Then I heard all of them laughing
Mum, Dad, the lady from number fifty-seven
And you
I was so unsure of what was happening
Were they laughing because they were so happy
That you were still alive?
That all was well?

And slowly I realised
It was a joke
A stupid joke

   Silence

PHOEBE *hangs her head*

CAROLINE *walks over and tenderly places a kiss on the top of her head*

Moments pass

CAROLINE *sits down next to her*

Will she stay or will she go?

Maybe in the happier version she does invite Paul to Sunset Strip

Maybe he comes, maybe there's a different life for all

Hope springs eternal

Then as if to prove that point ...

SCENE FOUR

Before the lights go down

We see DAD *at his fish tank—and again he attempts to coax his fish into playing a tune on the glockenspiel*

This time the fish actually pulls the cord a few times and the tune is rung out

The tune should be recognisable

The first bars of 'Greensleeves'

Or

Something similar

DAD *is delighted, throws his arms into the air triumphantly*

Does he call out? Dance? Sing along?

He is proud of his fish, offers it the food reward it richly deserves, and yet ... while thrilled, he is also smug in his knowledge that he always knew it would be possible!

THE END

[ ] the
uncertainty
principle

GRIFFIN INDEPENDENT

THE UNCERTAINTY PRINCIPLE AND
GRIFFIN INDEPENDENT PRESENT

SUNSET STRIP
BY SUZIE MILLER
14 JUNE - 1 JULY 2017

Director Anthony Skuse

Assistant Director Graeme McRae

Producers Kate Armstrong-Smith,
Laurence Rosier Staines

Set and Costume Designer Emma Vine

Lighting and Projection Designer
Verity Hampson

Sound Designer and Composer
Benjamin Freeman

Stage Manager Gayda de Mesa

With Emma Jackson, Simon Lyndon,
Lex Marinos, Georgina Symes

SBW STABLES THEATRE
14 JUNE - 1 JULY

Production Sponsor

Government Partners

McGrath
foundation

Australian Government

Australia
Council
for the Arts

NSW
GOVERNMENT | Arts
NSW

Griffin acknowledges the generosity of the Seaborn, Broughton & Walford Foundation
in allowing it the use of the SBW Stables Theatre rent free, less outgoings, since 1986.

PLAYWRIGHT'S NOTES
SUZIE MILLER

I should preface this with an apology for its length, but there is so much to say about the unique place of Australian theatre, especially in light of government funding cuts. So too is there much to say about the love, generosity and commitment that was brought to bear on this production. The coming together of people, funds, artists and foundations.

Sunset Strip is a play about people who happen to be in a few shitty situations. I wanted it to reflect how we bumble through life with all sorts of challenges, some of which will never be fixed or cured, but which we take on board and battle along with. There are also many funny and darkly ironic moments that come about even when we live with 'everything going wrong'. I wanted to celebrate this because it is something we have all known and have experienced. I have sat with my darling mum through chemo and hospitals this last year, and boy have we had some crazy laughs amongst the tears.

And then there is *hope*. Human beings are remarkable at finding hope in the hardest and most unlikely places. Strangely it is this mixture of hope and horror that drew me to the world of this play. Because in being lost, ill, getting old, having cancer, melting down or screwing up, we are at our most human, and sometimes that's the place where the best laughs are. We seem to intuitively know that. We bond over something that is bizarre even in the midst of the most challenging moments.

Sunset Strip is also about family, and how we are all so imperfect yet strangely imperfect in our own vulnerable and unique ways. I wanted to write a play that works on all stages —both large and small—and that spoke to all of us living our busy lives. That the play in its premiere season is on at Griffin—so intimate, so real, so filled with hope for the future of Australian theatre—felt fitting and in keeping with the themes.

I especially wanted to write a play that had two strong women characters at front and centre; they are the main story of this play. And so I make no apologies for the very female nature of the storytelling—how women talk, relate and move through life. Indeed I fully embrace and celebrate it. Historically playwrights do not put women as the main protagonists in their work. Research has shown that if you do it is harder to have the play programmed, and so the particularly female experiences do not often grace the stages. There is a unique humour about women together, the way we laugh and love and get angry all at the same time. But the male characters in this play are also fundamental to the telling of the story. Everyone in *Sunset Strip* is confronting their own fears.

My wonderfully talented collaborator Anthony Skuse has again taken a new play of mine into rehearsal and cast it with world class actors. I have watched as the actors embody these characters in a manner that has just blown my mind. They have found vulnerabilities, love, anger, faults, strengths, crazy humour and ultimately, hope.

On an unremarkable Monday night in Sydney, a dear friend of mine, Sam Mostyn, who has always supported the arts, hosted a fundraiser at her home to see if we could raise funds to fully realise this independent production of *Sunset Strip*. With the issue of government arts funding weighing heavily on the shoulders of all artists, it was a great joy to see this group of fabulous people come together. Lee Lewis, in her enthusiastic manner, explained how hard it is to get financial support for theatre, how important Australian stories are; Kate Armstrong-Smith described the difference in watching an indie show compared to one that is fully funded—something we in the industry know, but do the audience? Those guests opened their hearts and generously supported this production to make it what it is today. The McGrath Foundation has come on board as supporters and as the beneficiaries of the proceeds of the printed script. We are supporting a new young woman playwright, Lotte Beckett, who has written a play with women as its main protagonists.

Griffin Theatre will host the moved reading of her work during the season of *Sunset Strip*. There is a lot of love and goodwill in this production. It makes me proud of my community.

Sunset Strip was one of those plays that in retrospect had obviously lived in my subconscious for a while. I lost a beloved aunt from breast cancer when I was 10 years old. It was not spoken about much, this tragedy that my father's family suffered terribly over. It frightened me, all the silence around it. Since that time I have lived with so many of my loved ones being touched by breast cancer—friends, family, colleagues, schoolmates, parents of my children's friends and more. I have sat in chemo rooms and by hospital beds and had some tears, life-changing conversations, and (bizarrely enough) incredible laughs. I wanted to write a play that reflected the fact that living and dealing with cancer is all about us. We just take it on board, fight the awfulness of the process, and embrace the human insights that it brings. Like most things in life, we don't have a manual for how to deal with it.

I wanted to show how we can often laugh in the face of adversity, find the ridiculous in it all. I wanted to explore what it means for women to bumble along, juggling their lives amongst it all. A sister, a friend, a nurse, can be a source of great love, support and just a hand to hold.

Anthony Skuse and I forged a creative relationship when Griffin partnered us up for my play *Caress/Ache* in 2015. He is a gentleman of sincere proportions, a delight to work with; I have been privy to his wisdom, humour, fierce intelligence, theatrical talents and commitment. Kate Armstrong-Smith (Executive Producer) and Laurence Rosier-Staines (Producer) have embraced this project with their skills and their love, and it shows. Emma Jackson has played in many of my early works, including my first foray to the Sydney Opera House and a show we took to Edinburgh. She remains something of a muse for me and again she nails it. The other actors I am working with for the first time. Georgina Symes carries a humanity in her work that layers her character with so much that is real; Simon Lyndon takes the character of Teddy and lights up the stage; and Lex Marinos' clarity and protection of his own character—a frail father losing his grip on reality— takes centre stage when we least expect it.

Aside from all the amazing donors, I need to thank Lee Lewis and all at Griffin Theatre especially Will, Estelle and Elliott who have been on the day-to-day email chain; Claire Grady and Currency Press who are always a playwright's best friend, my agent Dayne Kelly at RGM; and my dearest friends 'The Lisas', Sam Mostyn, Rochelle Zurnamer, Karen O'Connell and Nic Abadee; and huge thanks to the theatre people who helped this production along: Darlo Drama, Glenn Terry, Belinda Mason (photographer) Caleb Lewis, Joe Couch, Sofia & Sage Armstrong-Couch and Trish Wadley (UK).

To my family: Elaine and Rob Miller, and Robert, Gabriel and Sasha: it is you lot that I owe the most thanks to, I am always supported in doing a job I adore

DIRECTOR'S NOTES
ANTHONY SKUSE

I'm always intrigued to discover the echoes or residue of other works in a particular piece of art, be it a painting, a novel or a play. I listen out for them. Along with those constant questions that drive the playwright mad—why this decision, why these words and not those—the echoes alert me to qualities in the work that I might otherwise miss. They throw open the work like a tablecloth. Of course, they are not always intentional on the part of the artist playwright. They are also echoes of my particular experience of the world. Either way, they are there if I listen.

For me Suzie's language and poetry is redolent of the work of Dorothy Hewett, another Australian poet and playwright. There is a similar sensitivity to people in a landscape. The play's setting is one of those 'corrugated towns smelling of saltlake water'.[1] The characters are stranded on the edge of a dried-up lake, waiting. The endless expanse of earth becomes the site of language as they wait for the arrival of the children and death. Language is their conciliation.

New plays are wrought on the rehearsal room floor and the experience can be terrifying and exhilarating in equal measure. The dimensions of the stage are marked out with green tape and it seems impossibly small to suggest the open vistas of Sunset Strip. Everyone has to be prepared to fail spectacularly.

The playwright's intuitive choices are scrutinised and tested and, more often than not, solutions lead to further questions and uncertainty. But it's only when language has been transformed by action that the nature of each sequence can be revealed. The process requires patience, generosity, curiosity, deep listening, and courage from everyone. Suzie Miller brings these qualities to the room in spades. Her willingness to embrace the awkwardness of the rehearsal process makes her a great collaborator.

I imagine everyone will find echoes of their own family in *Sunset Strip*, especially in the characters' ability to find joy in the bleakest of situations. The play opens with a homecoming—a trope laden with echoes. Characters reach across a shared past to an uncertain future. The chess game at the end of the play, another of those echoes, suggests some sort of concord may yet be reached. But rather than two lovers in a cave, looking over the board are two of the play's most broken characters: Ray and Teddy. If there is to be any sense of reconciliation then it is still very far away, and 'the hardest and most difficult part [is] only beginning.'[2]

[1] Dorothy Hewett, 'Yealering in the Mind', published in *Wheatlands*, Fremantle Arts Centre Press, 2000
[2] Anton Chekhov, *The lady with the lap dog*, first published 1900

SUNSET STRIP DONORS

We thank you all.

FINANCIAL DONORS:

Sam Mostyn

Lisa Hunt & Lisa Pears

Suzanne Young

Kate Morgan & Richard McHugh

Richard Weinstein & Richard Benedict

Sally Herman

Belinda Gibson

Kevin Conner

Simeon & Lotte Beckett

Brigitte Markovic & Jonathan Kay Hoyle

Nicole Abadee & Robert MacFarlan

Bridget Fair

Sally Evans

Jeremy Kirk

Holly Kramer

Christine McLoughlin

Julia Pincus & Ian Learmonth

Kathleen Gilbert

Cass & Nick O'Connor

Penny Graham

Catherine West

IN-KIND DONORS:

Darlo Drama

Louise Walsh

Belinda Mason

Joe Couch

Sofia & Sage Armstrong-Couch

ACKNOWLEDGEMENTS

Donors, cast, crew and all others involved would like to acknowledge friends and family who have lived with breast cancer, and those who have supported them:

Kath Varley

Lyn Pears

Estelle Lee

Diana Hunter

Penny Graham

Kerrie-Anne McGrath

Kate Armstrong-Smith's aunt, Marilyn Armstrong

Pato Salmon

Ella Brown

Edwina Hundt

Cass & Nick's mum, Gay O'Connor

Jo Lucas

Anne Fallon

Kate Morgan's besties, Neâ Saunders and Ruth Morgan

Holly's mum, Marilyn Kramer, and good friend, Alex Wansey

Anneke Twigg

A close colleague of Georgina Syme's

Emma Jackson's friends, Flick Bush and Amanda

Richard Weinstein's dear friend—a survivor in Palm Beach

Jane Mahoney's longest friend (with whom she shared a boarding school in Ireland with the Benedictine nuns!), Shusannah Morris, and Shusannah's amazing support network of nurses, family and friends

Lex Marinos' aunts, Rean Roberts and Elaine Karophilis

Cabrini Hospital, Brighton, Victoria and the chemo nurses, especially Susan

Sydney Breast Cancer Foundation

The amazing breast care nurses at Chris O'Brien Lifehouse Breast Unit—Ruth, Anne and Kate

Suzie Miller's beloved sister-in-law, Rebecca Miller, and mother-in-law, Joan Beech-Jones

Suzie Miller's Aunty Wendy (who was lost at 27 years), Aunty Kaye and Nana Patricia Lilian Miller

The wonderful breast cancer nurses at the Mater Hospital, Sydney, who make time for all: Clare John (survivor and mentor), Michiko Ban and Alice Gibson

Heather Mitchell – superstar actor, mother, friend and the warmest person on earth!

Edwina Parsons, who delights us all with her good humour and kindness

Jane McGrath

The McGrath Foundation breast care nurses all around the country

Through the character of Ray we would also like to acknowledge those we love who have lived with dementia or Alzheimer's disease:

Nevell Fleming Skuse

Robert Young

Suzie Miller

Playwright

Suzie Miller is a multi-award winning British/Australian playwright. She is a graduate of the National Institute of Dramatic Art Australia, and has an MA from UNSW in Theatre, an Honours in Science and a Masters of Law. Miller has been in residence at National Theatre of Scotland (2014), National Theatre in London (2011, 2009), Griffin Theatre Sydney (2012), Ransom Theatre in Ireland (2009), Critical Stages NSW (2013), Theatre Gargantua Toronto (2013), and La Boite Theatre (2015, 2016). She was attached to to Ex Machina Quebec with Robert Lepage (2012) and has been commissioned by companies in Australia, England, Scotland and Canada.

Miller has had over 35 productions of her works staged in theatres and festivals in Australia, the UK, Ireland, Canada, London and New York. Recent shows include: *Snow White* (Queensland Opera / La Boite Theatre / Brisbane Festival); *DUST* (Black Swan Theatre Company) which won the WA Premier's Literary Award for Script; *Caress/Ache* (Griffin Theatre Company); *onefivezeroseven* (Perth International Arts Festival (PIAF)); *Driving Into Walls* (PIAF / Sydney Opera House); *The Sacrifice Zone* (Theatre Gargantua Toronto); *Overexposed* (WA State Theatre); and *Medea* (La Boite Theatre). In 2017 her play *Velvet Evening Séance* will premiere and tour Scotland, including the Edinburgh Fringe Festival. Her new work for 2018 is *The Mathematics of Longing* (La Boite Theatre).

Suzie has won the WA Premier's Literary Award for Script; the Kit Denton Fellowship; an AWGIE; Best New Play (Irish Times); and the New York Fringe Festival's Overall Excellence Award for Outstanding Playwriting. Productions of her plays have won nine Actors' Equity awards and various Helpmann awards.

Miller sits on the theatre committee of the Australian Writers' Guild and the boards of various theatre companies.

Anthony Skuse
Director
Anthony is a director, dramaturge and teacher. His directing credits include: *Caress/Ache* (Griffin Theatre Company); *Shabbat Dinner* (Rock Surfers); *Platonov* (ATYP Selects); *Constellations* (Darlinghurst Theatre Company), which received four Sydney Theatre Award nominations; *Realism* (WAAPA); *Stop Kiss* (Unlikely Productions); *The Voices Project* and *The Greek Project: Aischylos, Euripides and Sophocles* (ATYP); *On the Shore of the Wide World* (Griffin Independent) which received two Sydney Theatre Award nominations; *4000 Miles* (Under the Wharf / La Boite), which received two Sydney Theatre Award nominations; *Punk Rock* (Under the Wharf) which won three Sydney Theatre Awards; *Dioclesian* (Pinchgut Opera); *Bug, References to Salvador Dali Make Me Hot, The Cold Child* and *Live Acts On Stage* (Griffin Independent); *Bad Jazz, pool (no water)* and *Terrorism* (Darlinghurst Theatre); *Too Young For Ghosts* and *Bright Room Called Day* (NIDA). Anthony is Head of Performance at Actors Centre Australia, where he has been on staff since 1994. He has also taught at Sydney's College of Fine Arts and NIDA, where he was an Associate Lecturer for Performance Practices and taught Repertoire with Playwrights from 2009 to 2012.

Graeme McRae
Assistant Director
Graeme is a founding member of pantsguys Productions. As an actor his work for stage includes *Three Sisters* (Sport For Jove); *Space Cats the Musical* (Brevity Theatre); *Coming To See Aunt Sophie* (Blumenthal Productions); *Platonov* (Mophead Productions); *The Gruffalo* (CDP); *On the Shore of the Wide World, Sweet Nothings, The Shape of Things, autobahn* and *Punk Rock* (pantsguys Productions) for which he won a Sydney Theatre Award. As director: *Oh, the Humanity* (pantsguys Productions) and as assistant director: *Between the Streetlight and the Moon* (Mophead Productions).

Kate Armstrong-Smith

Exectutive Producer

Kate supports and realises independent choreographers' and directors' works. She has worked in development with festivals including Good Vibrations, Adelaide Fringe, Adelaide Arts Festival, Indigenous Festivals of Australia and Sydney Festival. Kate worked to create the award-winning audience development scheme Fringe Benefits for the Adelaide Fringe and was awarded a Churchill Fellowship to investigate strategies to further engage new generations in the performing arts.

Laurence Rosier Staines

Producer

Laurence is a filmmaker, writer, producer and director. He created the web series and short film *Real Estate,* which has over 180K views and was film of the month at the Oasis Short Film Screening. Laurence's stage work has appeared at Blue Room Theatre, Tuxedo Cat, Giant Dwarf, Rock Surfers, Factory Theatre, Seymour Centre and 107 Projects. His screen work has been at Night of Horror IFF, SF3 Smartfone Flick Fest, Tucson Film & Music Festival, Pasadena IFF, Toronto Smartphone Film Festival, California International Shorts Festival, Viten Film Festival and more. In 2017 he was a PACT resident artist and created an immersive work for Underbelly Arts.

Emma Vine

Set and Costume Designer

Emma is a set and costume designer for theatre, opera, dance and film. A graduate of NIDA, during her final year Emma designed set and costume for Garry Stewart's *Choreography* at Carriageworks and costume for Stephen Sewell's *Kandahar Gate*. Her designs include costume for *Only Heaven Knows* (Hayes Theatre Company / Luckiest Productions), *The Turquoise Elephant* (Griffin), *Three Sisters* (Sport for Jove); set and costume for *The Mystery Of Love And Sex* (Darlinghurst Theatre Company); and set for *Heathers: The Musical* (national tour); *The Waiting Room, Water Angel* (Sydney Opera House); *The Voices Project* (ATYP); *Credeaux Canvas* (Seymour Centre); and co-design for *Klutz* (Brisbane Festival / NIDA). Film credits include production design for short film *Quietus*; and costume design for short film *The Fall*.

Verity Hampson

Lighting and Projection Designer

Verity is a NIDA graduate with over 10 years' experience as a lighting and projection designer. Verity has designed for over 90 theatre productions, working with some of Australia's most talented directors and choreographers. For television Verity has been a lighting director for the ABC's *Live at the Basement* and *The Roast*. Verity was awarded the Mike Walsh Fellowship in 2012 which took her to Broadway to work with projection designers 59 Productions. Verity was the winner of the 2013 Sydney Theatre Award for the best mainstage lighting design for her work on *Machinal* at the Sydney Theatre Company.

Benjamin Freeman

Sound Designer and Composer

Benjamin has been performing in the arts since an early age. He has been involved in over 30 theatre productions during the years including Stooged Theatre's *Rabbit and Rio Saki*, Tantrum Theatre's *Blackrock* (for which he received a CONDA for his role as Ricko), and ATYP's *Dwarf Revue.* He has performed in the Sydney Fringe since its inception in 2010. During the last few years Ben has focused on his music, playing with bands across many genres in the Sydney scene, doing session work at 301 Studios and completing an improvised piano album to be released later this year.

Gayda de Mesa

Stage Manager

Gayda graduated from the National Institute of Dramatic Arts (NIDA) with a Bachelor of Dramatic Arts (Production) and has spent the last 10 years working in technical production for theatre and live events. Her recent productions include *The Guru of Chai* (Indian Ink / Belvoir), *Cabaret* (David M. Hawkins Productions), *Big Fish* (Hayes Theatre Company / RPG Productions), the Melbourne International Comedy Festival, *Songs For A New World* (Blue Saint Productions), and *UNEND* (Never Never Theatre Company).

Emma Jackson

Phoebe

Emma's career has spanned theatre, film and TV since her graduation from NIDA. For QTC/Black Swan she recently appeared in *Once In Royal David's City*; for Belvoir, *The Blind Giant is Dancing*, *Food* (3 seasons, including National Tour) and *Fool for Love* (B Sharp / Savage Productions). She also performed in *The Long Way Home* (Sydney Theatre Company); *Nothing Personal* and *Let the Sunshine* (Ensemble Theatre); *Dead Man's Cellphone* (Melbourne Theatre Company); and *Stoning Mary* (Griffin Theatre). Emma won the Marten Bequest Travelling Scholarship in 2006 and relocated to New York to train with the SITI Co and intern with The Wooster Group. In the US, Emma appeared in *The Bird*, *Reader*, *Windows* and *Bed* (One Year Lease Theatre Company, New York); and *C4: The Chekhov Project* (Prospect Theatre, New York). She also performed in *Reasonable Doubt* (Theatre Tours International) in London and at the Edinburgh Festival. Screen credits include: *House of Bond* (Nine Network), *The Killing Field* (Seven Network), *Crownies* (ABC), *Killing Time* (Fremantle Media), and *The Alice & Rescue* (Southern Star).

Simon Lyndon

Teddy

Some of Simon's favourite roles so far include Ort in *That Eye, The Sky*, directed by Richard Roxburgh; Jared in *Blackrock* at STC and Ricko in the film adaptation; *Cloudstreet* at Belvoir, directed by Neil Armfield; and *Popcorn* for Black Swan. Simon has appeared in various TV and film productions over the years, including Terence Malick's *The Thin Red Line*, *Chopper*, *Blackrock*, *My Brother Jack*, *Cleo*, *Spirited*, *Deadline*, *Gallipoli* and *Underbelly*. Shortly after graduating from WAAPA in 1995, Simon was a founding member of Tamarama Rock Surfers. He directed their first Sydney production, *Road*, followed by *Diary of a Madman*. Simon has been nominated for AFI awards for *Blackrock* and *My Brother Jack*, and won the award for Best Supporting Actor with the role of Jimmy Loughlin in *Chopper*.

Lex Marinos
Ray

Lex Marinos OAM was born in Wagga Wagga, NSW into a family of Greek cafe owners. Lex attended the University of NSW, receiving a BA with Honours in Drama, and also studied with renowned American acting teacher Stella Adler. Since then he has worked in all areas of the entertainment industry as an actor, director, writer, broadcaster and teacher. He is best known for his television performances in *Kingswood Country* and ABC's production of *The Slap*, as well as other series, films and TV episodes, and countless stage productions. His work has taken him all over Australia, from remote Indigenous communities to the Opening Ceremony of the Sydney Olympics. Lex has also worked extensively on ABC radio since the riotous inception of 2JJ. Lex has held many advisory and governance positions with arts and cultural organizations including SOCOG, The Australia Council, and Community Broadcasting Foundation. His book *Blood and Circuses: an irresponsible memoir* was published by Allen & Unwin. He has been a proud member of Actors Equity since 1970.

Georgina Symes
Caroline

Georgina has performed with Sydney Theatre Company (STC), Queensland Theatre Company (QTC), Bell Shakespeare, Griffin and Darlinghurst Theatre Company. She toured the 20th anniversary production of *Away* and then took up an artist residency with QTC performing in *The Importance of Being Earnest*, *The Female of the Species*, *Ruby Moon*, and *Beckett x 3*. Other theatre credits include *The Alchemist* (national tour, Bell Shakespeare / QTC), *Deathtrap* and *Every Second* (Darlinghurst Theatre Company); *In a Heartbeat* (STC); *Porn.Cake*, *Crestfall* (Griffin); *The Dance of Jeremiah* (La Boite Theatre). Georgina's film and TV credits include indie feature films *The Tail Job* and *Bad Behaviour* and short films *Eaglehawk* and *Josh*. Recently she appeared in *Wham Bam Thank You Ma'am* (ABC / Skitbox)*, The Elegant Gentleman's Guide to Knife Fighting*, *Rake* and *Bananas in Pyjamas*. Her debut solo work *Uta Uber Kool Ja* had sellout seasons at fringe festivals nationally, winning Best Performance (Perth Fringe), the John Chataway Innovation Award (Adelaide Fringe) and the Tour Ready Award (Melbourne Fringe).

McGrath Foundation has supported 54,000 families.

Currently funds 117 Breast Care Nurses.*

THANK YOU

We're proud and excited and grateful to partner with 'Sunset Strip' – an incredible script, a powerful performance, and a devastatingly honest insight into one family affected by breast cancer, as well as dementia.

The McGrath Foundation makes life that little bit easier for families experiencing breast cancer, by placing specialist McGrath Breast Care Nurses in communities across Australia.

We believe that women and men diagnosed with breast cancer, and their families, need consistent, compassionate and expert support throughout their experience – wherever they live, **for free.**

But the need is growing – we desperately need **79 more**, to ensure that every family affected by breast cancer has access to this specialist support.

To find out more about us, or to contribute, visit **www.mcgrathfoundation.com.au**

McGrath Foundation

* June 2017

Visit Currency Press' website now to:

- Buy your books online
- Browse through our full list of titles, from plays to screenplays, books on theatre, film and music, and more
- Choose a play for your school or amateur performance group by cast size and gender
- Obtain information about performance rights
- Find out about theatre productions and other performing arts news across Australia
- For students, read our study guides
- For teachers, access syllabus and other relevant information
- Sign up for our email newsletter

The performing arts publisher

www.ingramcontent.com/pod-product-compliance
Lightning Source LLC
Chambersburg PA
CBHW050019090426
42734CB00021B/3338